Build Your Marriage®
One Day at a Time

Questions to Help You and Your
Spouse Connect at a Deeper Level

by
Brad and Heidi Mitchell

Published by

Build Your Marriage
BuildYourMarriage.org

For:
Robert & Leandra
Tovey & Andrew
Rachael & Cole

*We are thankful for the way each of you strives
to build your marriage with Jesus as the foundation.
We love you.*

Introduction

"To love at all is to be vulnerable." - C.S. Lewis

What if you knew your spouse so well that you could plan an experience they would be sure to enjoy? Or give them a gift they would love? Or serve them in a way that was helpful to them? Or understand their desires and thought processes? And, they would do the same for you? *Connecting deeply is vital to loving intimately.*

Several years ago we were driving down the interstate on one of our many road trips. To pass the time we decided to ask each other a question on any topic. Brad would ask a question and Heidi would answer it. Next, Brad would have to answer the question as well. Then it was Heidi's turn to ask a new question. This became a tradition for us. We realized that this exercise helped us grow in our knowledge and understanding of each other.

Most married couples want to grow in intimacy. They desire to know not only facts about their spouse, but why their spouse thinks or behaves a certain way. What factors shape their spouse's tastes and opinions? What motivates their spouse? What does their spouse like or dislike? What brings them joy?

To help couples build their marriage we created this question book. There's a question for every day of the year, and you can start at any time during the year. Each day has a question for both the husband and wife to answer. You can choose to answer verbally and talk about each question or you may prefer to write your answers in the book as a keepsake journal for the two of you. Perhaps you'll want to do a combination of both - talk about some questions and write some responses in the book. Our desire is that by devoting some time each day to this activity, you will connect deeply as you build your marriage one day at a time.

Day 1

What is your biggest regret in life?

Husband's answer:

_____

_____

_____

_____

_____

_____

_____

_____

_____

_____

Wife's answer:

_____

_____

_____

_____

_____

_____

_____

_____

_____

_____

Day 2

What have been the biggest joys in your life?

Husband's answer:

_____

_____

_____

_____

_____

_____

_____

_____

_____

_____

Wife's answer:

_____

_____

_____

_____

_____

_____

_____

_____

_____

_____

Day 3

Who is your favorite Bible character besides Jesus? Why?

Husband's answer:

_____
_____
_____
_____
_____
_____
_____
_____
_____
_____

Wife's answer:

_____
_____
_____
_____
_____
_____
_____
_____
_____
_____

Day 4

In what season of your life did you experience the greatest spiritual growth? Why?

Husband's answer:

_____

_____

_____

_____

_____

_____

_____

_____

_____

_____

Wife's answer:

_____

_____

_____

_____

_____

_____

_____

_____

_____

_____

Day 5

What is your favorite sport to watch?

Husband's answer:

_____
_____
_____
_____
_____
_____
_____
_____
_____
_____

Wife's answer:

_____
_____
_____
_____
_____
_____
_____
_____
_____
_____

Day 6

What is your favorite place that we've traveled together?

Husband's answer:

_____
_____
_____
_____
_____
_____
_____
_____
_____
_____

Wife's answer:

_____
_____
_____
_____
_____
_____
_____
_____
_____
_____

Day 7

What is one of your spouse's best qualities?

Husband's answer:

_____
_____
_____
_____
_____
_____
_____
_____
_____
_____

Wife's answer:

_____
_____
_____
_____
_____
_____
_____
_____
_____
_____

Day 8

What events or experiences have most impacted your life?

Husband's answer:

_____
_____
_____
_____
_____
_____
_____
_____
_____
_____

Wife's answer:

_____
_____
_____
_____
_____
_____
_____
_____
_____
_____

Day 9

What three qualities do you search for in a church home?

Husband's answer:

_____
_____
_____
_____
_____
_____
_____
_____
_____
_____

Wife's answer:

_____
_____
_____
_____
_____
_____
_____
_____
_____
_____

Day 10

Who is your closest friend? What do you like about them?

Husband's answer:

_____
_____
_____
_____
_____
_____
_____
_____
_____
_____

Wife's answer:

_____
_____
_____
_____
_____
_____
_____
_____
_____
_____

Day 11

What was your first job? Did you like it?

Husband's answer:

_____
_____
_____
_____
_____
_____
_____
_____
_____
_____

Wife's answer:

_____
_____
_____
_____
_____
_____
_____
_____
_____
_____

Day 12

What is something you'd like to try?

Husband's answer:

_____
_____
_____
_____
_____
_____
_____
_____
_____
_____

Wife's answer:

_____
_____
_____
_____
_____
_____
_____
_____
_____
_____

Day 13

If you could replace something in your home, what would it be?

Husband's answer:

_____

_____

_____

_____

_____

_____

_____

_____

_____

Wife's answer:

_____

_____

_____

_____

_____

_____

_____

_____

_____

Day 14

What nature or outdoor sound do you enjoy?

Husband's answer:

_____

_____

_____

_____

_____

_____

_____

_____

_____

Wife's answer:

_____

_____

_____

_____

_____

_____

_____

_____

_____

Day 15

What value is uncompromising for you?

Husband's answer:

_____
_____
_____
_____
_____
_____
_____
_____
_____
_____

Wife's answer:

_____
_____
_____
_____
_____
_____
_____
_____
_____
_____

Day 16

When was the last time you were frustrated with your spouse? Why?

Husband's answer:

_____
_____
_____
_____
_____
_____
_____
_____
_____
_____

Wife's answer:

_____
_____
_____
_____
_____
_____
_____
_____
_____
_____

Day 17

What is the last thing you purchased for yourself?

Husband's answer:

_____
_____
_____
_____
_____
_____
_____
_____
_____
_____
_____

Wife's answer:

_____
_____
_____
_____
_____
_____
_____
_____
_____
_____
_____

Day 18

What was your hardest day in the past year and why?

Husband's answer:

_____
_____
_____
_____
_____
_____
_____
_____
_____
_____

Wife's answer:

_____
_____
_____
_____
_____
_____
_____
_____
_____
_____

Day 19

What is the most joyful moment we've had as a couple?

Husband's answer:

_____
_____
_____
_____
_____
_____
_____
_____
_____
_____

Wife's answer:

_____
_____
_____
_____
_____
_____
_____
_____
_____
_____

Day 20

What is your favorite candy?

Husband's answer:

_____
_____
_____
_____
_____
_____
_____
_____
_____
_____

Wife's answer:

_____
_____
_____
_____
_____
_____
_____
_____
_____
_____

Day 21

Are there any parts of the Bible you wrestle with? How?

Husband's answer:

_____
_____
_____
_____
_____
_____
_____
_____
_____
_____

Wife's answer:

_____
_____
_____
_____
_____
_____
_____
_____
_____
_____

Day 22

Besides retirement, what do you look forward to as we grow old together?

Husband's answer:

_____
_____
_____
_____
_____
_____
_____
_____
_____
_____

Wife's answer:

_____
_____
_____
_____
_____
_____
_____
_____
_____
_____

Day 23

What false expectations did you have entering marriage?

Husband's answer:

_____
_____
_____
_____
_____
_____
_____
_____
_____
_____

Wife's answer:

_____
_____
_____
_____
_____
_____
_____
_____
_____
_____

Day 24

What do you think your life's purpose is?

Husband's answer:

_____
_____
_____
_____
_____
_____
_____
_____
_____
_____

Wife's answer:

_____
_____
_____
_____
_____
_____
_____
_____
_____
_____

Day 25

Pick a couple with whom you are friends. How can we be better friends to them?

Husband's answer:

_____

_____

_____

_____

_____

_____

_____

_____

_____

_____

Wife's answer:

_____

_____

_____

_____

_____

_____

_____

_____

_____

_____

Day 26

When did a co-worker let you down? How did you respond?

Husband's answer:

_____

_____

_____

_____

_____

_____

_____

_____

_____

Wife's answer:

_____

_____

_____

_____

_____

_____

_____

_____

_____

Day 27

What hopes and dreams do you have for our children?

Husband's answer:

_____
_____
_____
_____
_____
_____
_____
_____
_____
_____

Wife's answer:

_____
_____
_____
_____
_____
_____
_____
_____
_____
_____

Day 28

If you had a day alone in your house, how would you spend it?

Husband's answer:

_____
_____
_____
_____
_____
_____
_____
_____
_____
_____

Wife's answer:

_____
_____
_____
_____
_____
_____
_____
_____
_____
_____

Day 29

What was the most beautiful nature scene you've ever experienced?

Husband's answer:

_____

_____

_____

_____

_____

_____

_____

_____

_____

Wife's answer:

_____

_____

_____

_____

_____

_____

_____

_____

_____

Day 30

What is your biggest failure?

Husband's answer:

_____
_____
_____
_____
_____
_____
_____
_____
_____
_____

Wife's answer:

_____
_____
_____
_____
_____
_____
_____
_____
_____
_____

Day 31

In what areas of your life are you content?

Husband's answer:

_____
_____
_____
_____
_____
_____
_____
_____
_____
_____

Wife's answer:

_____
_____
_____
_____
_____
_____
_____
_____
_____
_____

Day 32

What was your favorite childhood activity?

Husband's answer:

_____
_____
_____
_____
_____
_____
_____
_____
_____
_____

Wife's answer:

_____
_____
_____
_____
_____
_____
_____
_____
_____
_____

Day 33

What do you think your top two or three spiritual gifts are?

Husband's answer:

_____

_____

_____

_____

_____

_____

_____

_____

_____

_____

Wife's answer:

_____

_____

_____

_____

_____

_____

_____

_____

_____

_____

Day 34

What is your favorite thing to do in your spare time?

Husband's answer:

_____
_____
_____
_____
_____
_____
_____
_____
_____

Wife's answer:

_____
_____
_____
_____
_____
_____
_____
_____
_____

Day 35

How would you describe your dream home?

Husband's answer:

_____
_____
_____
_____
_____
_____
_____
_____
_____
_____

Wife's answer:

_____
_____
_____
_____
_____
_____
_____
_____
_____
_____

Day 36

What person has had a profound impact on your life?

Husband's answer:

_____
_____
_____
_____
_____
_____
_____
_____
_____
_____

Wife's answer:

_____
_____
_____
_____
_____
_____
_____
_____
_____
_____

Day 37

What is your favorite part of your job? Why?

Husband's answer:

_____
_____
_____
_____
_____
_____
_____
_____
_____
_____

Wife's answer:

_____
_____
_____
_____
_____
_____
_____
_____
_____
_____

Day 38

Have you ever been issued a traffic ticket? For what violation?

Husband's answer:

_____

_____

_____

_____

_____

_____

_____

_____

_____

_____

Wife's answer:

_____

_____

_____

_____

_____

_____

_____

_____

_____

_____

Day 39

Who would you most like to have for a neighbor?

Husband's answer:

_____
_____
_____
_____
_____
_____
_____
_____
_____
_____
_____

Wife's answer:

_____
_____
_____
_____
_____
_____
_____
_____
_____
_____
_____

Day 40

What is your perspective on tithing our income (giving God 10%)? Why?

Husband's answer:

_____

_____

_____

_____

_____

_____

_____

_____

_____

_____

Wife's answer:

_____

_____

_____

_____

_____

_____

_____

_____

_____

_____

Day 41

When was the last time you forgave someone? For what?

Husband's answer:

_____
_____
_____
_____
_____
_____
_____
_____
_____
_____

Wife's answer:

_____
_____
_____
_____
_____
_____
_____
_____
_____
_____

Day 42

What is one thing you admire about your grandparents?

Husband's answer:

_____
_____
_____
_____
_____
_____
_____
_____
_____
_____

Wife's answer:

_____
_____
_____
_____
_____
_____
_____
_____
_____
_____

Day 43

What style of music do you like best?

Husband's answer:

_____

_____

_____

_____

_____

_____

_____

_____

_____

_____

Wife's answer:

_____

_____

_____

_____

_____

_____

_____

_____

_____

_____

Day 44

How can we best defend our marriage against Satan's attacks?

Husband's answer:

_____
_____
_____
_____
_____
_____
_____
_____
_____
_____

Wife's answer:

_____
_____
_____
_____
_____
_____
_____
_____
_____
_____

Day 45

How can we be more sexually intimate?

Husband's answer:

_____

_____

_____

_____

_____

_____

_____

_____

_____

_____

Wife's answer:

_____

_____

_____

_____

_____

_____

_____

_____

_____

_____

Day 46

Who do you think could be a good friend for you that you haven't pursued?

Husband's answer:

_____
_____
_____
_____
_____
_____
_____
_____
_____
_____

Wife's answer:

_____
_____
_____
_____
_____
_____
_____
_____
_____
_____

Day 47

Did you ever write in a journal or diary?

Husband's answer:

_____

_____

_____

_____

_____

_____

_____

_____

_____

Wife's answer:

_____

_____

_____

_____

_____

_____

_____

_____

_____

Day 48

What struggle are you facing right now?

Husband's answer:

_____
_____
_____
_____
_____
_____
_____
_____
_____
_____

Wife's answer:

_____
_____
_____
_____
_____
_____
_____
_____
_____
_____

Day 49

In the last month, what brought you the greatest joy?

Husband's answer:

_____
_____
_____
_____
_____
_____
_____
_____
_____
_____

Wife's answer:

_____
_____
_____
_____
_____
_____
_____
_____
_____
_____

Day 50

What is your favorite name for God (e.g. Emanuel, Prince of Peace, Abba Father, etc.)?

Husband's answer:

_____

_____

_____

_____

_____

_____

_____

_____

_____

_____

Wife's answer:

_____

_____

_____

_____

_____

_____

_____

_____

_____

_____

Day 51

Where do you think we may have an imbalance of household responsibilities? How can we solve that?

Husband's answer:

_____
_____
_____
_____
_____
_____
_____
_____
_____
_____
_____

Wife's answer:

_____
_____
_____
_____
_____
_____
_____
_____
_____
_____
_____

Day 52

What is the best thing that happened at your job this week?

Husband's answer:

_____
_____
_____
_____
_____
_____
_____
_____
_____
_____

Wife's answer:

_____
_____
_____
_____
_____
_____
_____
_____
_____
_____

Day 53

Are you an optimist, realist, or pessimist? Why?

Husband's answer:

_____
_____
_____
_____
_____
_____
_____
_____
_____
_____

Wife's answer:

_____
_____
_____
_____
_____
_____
_____
_____
_____
_____

Day 54

What do you like about your neighborhood?

Husband's answer:

_____
_____
_____
_____
_____
_____
_____
_____
_____

Wife's answer:

_____
_____
_____
_____
_____
_____
_____
_____
_____

Day 55

Have you ever been mad at God? When?

Husband's answer:

_____
_____
_____
_____
_____
_____
_____
_____
_____
_____

Wife's answer:

_____
_____
_____
_____
_____
_____
_____
_____
_____
_____

Day 56

What comes to mind when you look at your wedding ring?

Husband's answer:

_____
_____
_____
_____
_____
_____
_____
_____
_____
_____

Wife's answer:

_____
_____
_____
_____
_____
_____
_____
_____
_____
_____

Day 57

What has been your most fulfilling job? Why?

Husband's answer:

_____
_____
_____
_____
_____
_____
_____
_____
_____
_____

Wife's answer:

_____
_____
_____
_____
_____
_____
_____
_____
_____
_____

Day 58

What is your favorite sport to participate in?

Husband's answer:

_____
_____
_____
_____
_____
_____
_____
_____
_____
_____

Wife's answer:

_____
_____
_____
_____
_____
_____
_____
_____
_____
_____

Day 59

How can we incorporate God more into our everyday
lives?

Husband's answer:

_____
_____
_____
_____
_____
_____
_____
_____
_____
_____

Wife's answer:

_____
_____
_____
_____
_____
_____
_____
_____
_____
_____

Day 60

How can you be a better listener in your marriage?

Husband's answer:

_____
_____
_____
_____
_____
_____
_____
_____
_____
_____

Wife's answer:

_____
_____
_____
_____
_____
_____
_____
_____
_____
_____

Day 61

If you could take a class on any subject, what would you choose?

Husband's answer:

_____
_____
_____
_____
_____
_____
_____
_____
_____

Wife's answer:

_____
_____
_____
_____
_____
_____
_____
_____
_____

Day 62

What was your most cherished childhood possession?

Husband's answer:

_____
_____
_____
_____
_____
_____
_____
_____
_____
_____

Wife's answer:

_____
_____
_____
_____
_____
_____
_____
_____
_____
_____

Day 63

What is your favorite quality of Jesus?

Husband's answer:

_____
_____
_____
_____
_____
_____
_____
_____
_____
_____

Wife's answer:

_____
_____
_____
_____
_____
_____
_____
_____
_____
_____

Day 64

What is something you wish your spouse would throw (or give) away?

Husband's answer:

_____
_____
_____
_____
_____
_____
_____
_____
_____
_____

Wife's answer:

_____
_____
_____
_____
_____
_____
_____
_____
_____
_____

Day 65

What have you lied about? Did you ever confess?

Husband's answer:

_____
_____
_____
_____
_____
_____
_____
_____
_____
_____

Wife's answer:

_____
_____
_____
_____
_____
_____
_____
_____
_____
_____

Day 66

What do you think is your spouse's favorite article of clothing?

Husband's answer:

_____
_____
_____
_____
_____
_____
_____
_____
_____
_____

Wife's answer:

_____
_____
_____
_____
_____
_____
_____
_____
_____
_____

Day 67

When you look at your spouse, what is the first thing you notice?

Husband's answer:

_____

_____

_____

_____

_____

_____

_____

_____

_____

_____

Wife's answer:

_____

_____

_____

_____

_____

_____

_____

_____

_____

_____

Day 68

Do you like change or not? Why?

Husband's answer:

_____
_____
_____
_____
_____
_____
_____
_____
_____
_____

Wife's answer:

_____
_____
_____
_____
_____
_____
_____
_____
_____
_____

Day 69

What is something you've prayed for fervently?

Husband's answer:

_____
_____
_____
_____
_____
_____
_____
_____
_____
_____

Wife's answer:

_____
_____
_____
_____
_____
_____
_____
_____
_____
_____

Day 70

What concerns do you have for our children?

Husband's answer:

_____
_____
_____
_____
_____
_____
_____
_____
_____
_____

Wife's answer:

_____
_____
_____
_____
_____
_____
_____
_____
_____
_____

Day 71

What is something your spouse doesn't know about you?

Husband's answer:

_____
_____
_____
_____
_____
_____
_____
_____
_____
_____

Wife's answer:

_____
_____
_____
_____
_____
_____
_____
_____
_____
_____

Day 72

Have you ever experienced a spiritual wilderness or "dry" time? What was it like for you?

Husband's answer:

_____
_____
_____
_____
_____
_____
_____
_____
_____
_____

Wife's answer:

_____
_____
_____
_____
_____
_____
_____
_____
_____
_____

Day 73

What trait do you admire in your spouse?

Husband's answer:

_____
_____
_____
_____
_____
_____
_____
_____
_____

Wife's answer:

_____
_____
_____
_____
_____
_____
_____
_____
_____

Day 74

Do you compare yourself to other people? If so, in what area of your life?

Husband's answer:

_____
_____
_____
_____
_____
_____
_____
_____
_____
_____

Wife's answer:

_____
_____
_____
_____
_____
_____
_____
_____
_____
_____

Day 75

What are some ways we've seen God work in our lives and marriage?

Husband's answer:

_____
_____
_____
_____
_____
_____
_____
_____
_____
_____

Wife's answer:

_____
_____
_____
_____
_____
_____
_____
_____
_____
_____

Day 76

Are you satisfied with the way we celebrate holidays?

Husband's answer:

_____
_____
_____
_____
_____
_____
_____
_____
_____
_____

Wife's answer:

_____
_____
_____
_____
_____
_____
_____
_____
_____
_____

Day 77

How can we be more affectionate as a couple?

Husband's answer:

_____
_____
_____
_____
_____
_____
_____
_____
_____
_____

Wife's answer:

_____
_____
_____
_____
_____
_____
_____
_____
_____
_____

Day 78

What is your opinion of New Year's resolutions? Do you make them?

Husband's answer:

_____
_____
_____
_____
_____
_____
_____
_____
_____
_____

Wife's answer:

_____
_____
_____
_____
_____
_____
_____
_____
_____
_____

Day 79

What is one aspect of your parent's marriage that you admire and why?

Husband's answer:

_____
_____
_____
_____
_____
_____
_____
_____
_____
_____

Wife's answer:

_____
_____
_____
_____
_____
_____
_____
_____
_____
_____

Day 80

What was one of your best Christmas memories? Describe it.

Husband's answer:

_____
_____
_____
_____
_____
_____
_____
_____
_____
_____

Wife's answer:

_____
_____
_____
_____
_____
_____
_____
_____
_____
_____

Day 81

What qualities make a great husband?

Husband's answer:

_____
_____
_____
_____
_____
_____
_____
_____
_____
_____

Wife's answer:

_____
_____
_____
_____
_____
_____
_____
_____
_____
_____

Day 82

When have you felt the most lonely in your life?

Husband's answer:

_____
_____
_____
_____
_____
_____
_____
_____
_____
_____

Wife's answer:

_____
_____
_____
_____
_____
_____
_____
_____
_____
_____

Day 83

What differentiates your spouse from all others?

Husband's answer:

_____
_____
_____
_____
_____
_____
_____
_____
_____
_____

Wife's answer:

_____
_____
_____
_____
_____
_____
_____
_____
_____
_____

Day 84

When did someone make a wrong assumption about you?

Husband's answer:

_____
_____
_____
_____
_____
_____
_____
_____
_____
_____

Wife's answer:

_____
_____
_____
_____
_____
_____
_____
_____
_____
_____

Day 85

What is on your bucket list?

Husband's answer:

_____
_____
_____
_____
_____
_____
_____
_____
_____
_____

Wife's answer:

_____
_____
_____
_____
_____
_____
_____
_____
_____
_____

Day 86

When you think back to your wedding, is there anything you would do differently?

Husband's answer:

_____
_____
_____
_____
_____
_____
_____
_____
_____
_____

Wife's answer:

_____
_____
_____
_____
_____
_____
_____
_____
_____
_____

Day 87

Who were your closest childhood friends? What memories do you have with them?

Husband's answer:

_____
_____
_____
_____
_____
_____
_____
_____
_____
_____

Wife's answer:

_____
_____
_____
_____
_____
_____
_____
_____
_____
_____

Day 88

How have you pleasantly surprised your spouse in the past month?

Husband's answer:

_____
_____
_____
_____
_____
_____
_____
_____
_____
_____

Wife's answer:

_____
_____
_____
_____
_____
_____
_____
_____
_____
_____

Day 89

What financial goals do you have that we can work
toward achieving together?

Husband's answer:

_____

_____

_____

_____

_____

_____

_____

_____

_____

_____

Wife's answer:

_____

_____

_____

_____

_____

_____

_____

_____

_____

_____

Day 90

How can we communicate better?

Husband's answer:

_____

_____

_____

_____

_____

_____

_____

_____

_____

Wife's answer:

_____

_____

_____

_____

_____

_____

_____

_____

_____

Day 91

What are you reading? How has it affected you?

Husband's answer:

_____

_____

_____

_____

_____

_____

_____

_____

_____

_____

Wife's answer:

_____

_____

_____

_____

_____

_____

_____

_____

_____

_____

Day 92

How can we be proactive and protect our marriage from temptations?

Husband's answer:

_____

_____

_____

_____

_____

_____

_____

_____

_____

_____

Wife's answer:

_____

_____

_____

_____

_____

_____

_____

_____

_____

_____

Day 93

What is the biggest lesson you've learned in life?

Husband's answer:

_____
_____
_____
_____
_____
_____
_____
_____
_____
_____

Wife's answer:

_____
_____
_____
_____
_____
_____
_____
_____
_____
_____

Day 94

What has been one of the best things that happened in the past year?

Husband's answer:

_____
_____
_____
_____
_____
_____
_____
_____
_____
_____

Wife's answer:

_____
_____
_____
_____
_____
_____
_____
_____
_____
_____

Day 95

Do you have a favorite Bible story? What is it?

Husband's answer:

_____
_____
_____
_____
_____
_____
_____
_____
_____
_____

Wife's answer:

_____
_____
_____
_____
_____
_____
_____
_____
_____
_____

Day 96

What is one of the most memorable sermons you've heard? Why?

Husband's answer:

_____
_____
_____
_____
_____
_____
_____
_____
_____
_____

Wife's answer:

_____
_____
_____
_____
_____
_____
_____
_____
_____
_____

Day 97

If you could write a book, the title would be...

Husband's answer:

_____
_____
_____
_____
_____
_____
_____
_____
_____
_____

Wife's answer:

_____
_____
_____
_____
_____
_____
_____
_____
_____
_____

Day 98

What is the best trip you've ever taken? What did you enjoy about it?

Husband's answer:

_____
_____
_____
_____
_____
_____
_____
_____
_____
_____

Wife's answer:

_____
_____
_____
_____
_____
_____
_____
_____
_____
_____

Day 99

What will your spouse say is their favorite thing that you do in the mornings?

Husband's answer:

_____
_____
_____
_____
_____
_____
_____
_____
_____

Wife's answer:

_____
_____
_____
_____
_____
_____
_____
_____
_____

Day 100

Whose marriage do you admire and what do you like
about their marriage?

Husband's answer:

_____
_____
_____
_____
_____
_____
_____
_____
_____
_____

Wife's answer:

_____
_____
_____
_____
_____
_____
_____
_____
_____
_____

Day 101

Where would you like to serve on a missions trip?

Husband's answer:

_____
_____
_____
_____
_____
_____
_____
_____
_____
_____

Wife's answer:

_____
_____
_____
_____
_____
_____
_____
_____
_____
_____

Day 102

Which friends have you lost contact with that you miss?

Husband's answer:

_____
_____
_____
_____
_____
_____
_____
_____
_____
_____

Wife's answer:

_____
_____
_____
_____
_____
_____
_____
_____
_____
_____

Day 103

If you could live your life over again, would you choose the same vocation? If not, what career path would you follow?

Husband's answer:

_____
_____
_____
_____
_____
_____
_____
_____
_____
_____

Wife's answer:

_____
_____
_____
_____
_____
_____
_____
_____
_____
_____

Day 104

What quality is essential to be a great parent?

Husband's answer:

_____
_____
_____
_____
_____
_____
_____
_____
_____
_____
_____

Wife's answer:

_____
_____
_____
_____
_____
_____
_____
_____
_____
_____
_____

Day 105

Have you ever met anyone famous? Who?

Husband's answer:

_____
_____
_____
_____
_____
_____
_____
_____
_____
_____

Wife's answer:

_____
_____
_____
_____
_____
_____
_____
_____
_____
_____

Day 106

Where would you like to go on a walk or hike with your spouse?

Husband's answer:

_____
_____
_____
_____
_____
_____
_____
_____
_____
_____

Wife's answer:

_____
_____
_____
_____
_____
_____
_____
_____
_____
_____

Day 107

What is the bravest thing you've ever done?

Husband's answer:

_____
_____
_____
_____
_____
_____
_____
_____
_____
_____

Wife's answer:

_____
_____
_____
_____
_____
_____
_____
_____
_____
_____

Day 108

When was the last time you were angry with a family member? Why?

Husband's answer:

_____
_____
_____
_____
_____
_____
_____
_____
_____
_____

Wife's answer:

_____
_____
_____
_____
_____
_____
_____
_____
_____
_____

Day 109

When did you waste money? On what?

Husband's answer:

_____
_____
_____
_____
_____
_____
_____
_____
_____
_____

Wife's answer:

_____
_____
_____
_____
_____
_____
_____
_____
_____
_____

Day 110

What illness or disease scares you?

Husband's answer:

_____
_____
_____
_____
_____
_____
_____
_____
_____
_____

Wife's answer:

_____
_____
_____
_____
_____
_____
_____
_____
_____
_____

Day 111

What is the best thing your family of origin passed on to you?

Husband's answer:

_____
_____
_____
_____
_____
_____
_____
_____
_____
_____

Wife's answer:

_____
_____
_____
_____
_____
_____
_____
_____
_____
_____

Day 112

What is your favorite movie?

Husband's answer:

_____
_____
_____
_____
_____
_____
_____
_____
_____
_____

Wife's answer:

_____
_____
_____
_____
_____
_____
_____
_____
_____
_____

Day 113

What distracts you from following God more fully?

Husband's answer:

_____
_____
_____
_____
_____
_____
_____
_____
_____
_____

Wife's answer:

_____
_____
_____
_____
_____
_____
_____
_____
_____
_____

Day 114

Do you think we relax too much, not enough, or just the right amount of time? Why?

Husband's answer:

_____
_____
_____
_____
_____
_____
_____
_____
_____
_____

Wife's answer:

_____
_____
_____
_____
_____
_____
_____
_____
_____
_____

Day 115

Are you content with our level of physical fitness?

Husband's answer:

_____
_____
_____
_____
_____
_____
_____
_____
_____

Wife's answer:

_____
_____
_____
_____
_____
_____
_____
_____
_____

Day 116

Who has hurt you the most in life?

Husband's answer:

_____
_____
_____
_____
_____
_____
_____
_____
_____
_____

Wife's answer:

_____
_____
_____
_____
_____
_____
_____
_____
_____
_____

Day 117

Did you ever do something mischievous with your friends? What was it?

Husband's answer:

_____

_____

_____

_____

_____

_____

_____

_____

_____

_____

Wife's answer:

_____

_____

_____

_____

_____

_____

_____

_____

_____

_____

Day 118

Have you ever been fired or laid off? How did you react?

Husband's answer:

_____
_____
_____
_____
_____
_____
_____
_____
_____
_____

Wife's answer:

_____
_____
_____
_____
_____
_____
_____
_____
_____

Day 119

What type of surprises do you enjoy?

Husband's answer:

_____
_____
_____
_____
_____
_____
_____
_____
_____
_____

Wife's answer:

_____
_____
_____
_____
_____
_____
_____
_____
_____
_____

Day 120

If you could change any part of our home, what would it be?

Husband's answer:

_____
_____
_____
_____
_____
_____
_____
_____
_____
_____

Wife's answer:

_____
_____
_____
_____
_____
_____
_____
_____
_____
_____

Day 121

Are there any family traditions you would like to start?

Husband's answer:

_____
_____
_____
_____
_____
_____
_____
_____
_____
_____

Wife's answer:

_____
_____
_____
_____
_____
_____
_____
_____
_____
_____

Day 122

What makes you anxious?

Husband's answer:

_____
_____
_____
_____
_____
_____
_____
_____
_____
_____

Wife's answer:

_____
_____
_____
_____
_____
_____
_____
_____
_____
_____

Day 123

What did your parents do well?

Husband's answer:

_____
_____
_____
_____
_____
_____
_____
_____
_____
_____

Wife's answer:

_____
_____
_____
_____
_____
_____
_____
_____
_____
_____

Day 124

What are some of your favorite memories of us together?

Husband's answer:

_____
_____
_____
_____
_____
_____
_____
_____
_____
_____
_____

Wife's answer:

_____
_____
_____
_____
_____
_____
_____
_____
_____
_____
_____

Day 125

How is God using you?

Husband's answer:

_____

_____

_____

_____

_____

_____

_____

_____

_____

_____

Wife's answer:

_____

_____

_____

_____

_____

_____

_____

_____

_____

_____

Day 126

What is your ideal vacation?

Husband's answer:

_____
_____
_____
_____
_____
_____
_____
_____
_____
_____

Wife's answer:

_____
_____
_____
_____
_____
_____
_____
_____
_____
_____

Day 127

When did we laugh together?

Husband's answer:

_____
_____
_____
_____
_____
_____
_____
_____
_____
_____

Wife's answer:

_____
_____
_____
_____
_____
_____
_____
_____
_____
_____

Day 128

What famous person, living or dead, would you like to meet? Why?

Husband's answer:

_____

_____

_____

_____

_____

_____

_____

_____

_____

Wife's answer:

_____

_____

_____

_____

_____

_____

_____

_____

_____

Day 129

Do you want to advance in your career? Why or why not?

Husband's answer:

_____
_____
_____
_____
_____
_____
_____
_____
_____
_____

Wife's answer:

_____
_____
_____
_____
_____
_____
_____
_____
_____
_____

Day 130

What non-profit or charitable organization resonates with you?

Husband's answer:

_____

_____

_____

_____

_____

_____

_____

_____

_____

Wife's answer:

_____

_____

_____

_____

_____

_____

_____

_____

_____

Day 131

What is your favorite place you've ever lived? Why?

Husband's answer:

_____
_____
_____
_____
_____
_____
_____
_____
_____
_____

Wife's answer:

_____
_____
_____
_____
_____
_____
_____
_____
_____
_____

Day 132

Is there anything about your finances as a couple that creates stress for you?

Husband's answer:

_____
_____
_____
_____
_____
_____
_____
_____
_____
_____
_____

Wife's answer:

_____
_____
_____
_____
_____
_____
_____
_____
_____
_____

Day 133

What is the greatest loss you've ever faced?

Husband's answer:

_____
_____
_____
_____
_____
_____
_____
_____
_____
_____

Wife's answer:

_____
_____
_____
_____
_____
_____
_____
_____
_____
_____

Day 134

What is one of the best gifts you ever received?

Husband's answer:

_____

_____

_____

_____

_____

_____

_____

_____

_____

Wife's answer:

_____

_____

_____

_____

_____

_____

_____

_____

_____

Day 135

What is your favorite time of the day for us to be intimate?

Husband's answer:

_____
_____
_____
_____
_____
_____
_____
_____
_____
_____

Wife's answer:

_____
_____
_____
_____
_____
_____
_____
_____
_____
_____

Day 136

How do you think Satan attacks our marriage the most?

Husband's answer:

_____
_____
_____
_____
_____
_____
_____
_____
_____
_____

Wife's answer:

_____
_____
_____
_____
_____
_____
_____
_____
_____
_____

Day 137

What are some key lessons you learned from your parents growing up?

Husband's answer:

_____
_____
_____
_____
_____
_____
_____
_____
_____
_____

Wife's answer:

_____
_____
_____
_____
_____
_____
_____
_____
_____
_____

Day 138

What are two essential qualities of a good friend?

Husband's answer:

_____
_____
_____
_____
_____
_____
_____
_____
_____
_____

Wife's answer:

_____
_____
_____
_____
_____
_____
_____
_____
_____
_____

Day 139

What is something big in your life that you need to start or complete?

Husband's answer:

_____
_____
_____
_____
_____
_____
_____
_____
_____
_____

Wife's answer:

_____
_____
_____
_____
_____
_____
_____
_____
_____
_____

Day 140

When you think of your family heritage, what one thing would you like to change?

Husband's answer:

_____
_____
_____
_____
_____
_____
_____
_____
_____
_____

Wife's answer:

_____
_____
_____
_____
_____
_____
_____
_____
_____
_____

Day 141

When did you first decide God exists?

Husband's answer:

_____

_____

_____

_____

_____

_____

_____

_____

_____

_____

Wife's answer:

_____

_____

_____

_____

_____

_____

_____

_____

_____

_____

Day 142

What are some of the most memorable times we made love?

Husband's answer:

_____

_____

_____

_____

_____

_____

_____

_____

_____

Wife's answer:

_____

_____

_____

_____

_____

_____

_____

_____

_____

Day 143

What was your worst job? Why?

Husband's answer:

_____
_____
_____
_____
_____
_____
_____
_____
_____
_____
_____

Wife's answer:

_____
_____
_____
_____
_____
_____
_____
_____
_____
_____
_____

Day 144

What was your worst hairstyle?

Husband's answer:

_____
_____
_____
_____
_____
_____
_____
_____
_____
_____

Wife's answer:

_____
_____
_____
_____
_____
_____
_____
_____
_____
_____

Day 145

What makes you sad?

Husband's answer:

_____
_____
_____
_____
_____
_____
_____
_____
_____
_____
_____

Wife's answer:

_____
_____
_____
_____
_____
_____
_____
_____
_____
_____
_____

Day 146

What does Jesus mean to you?

Husband's answer:

_____

_____

_____

_____

_____

_____

_____

_____

_____

_____

Wife's answer:

_____

_____

_____

_____

_____

_____

_____

_____

_____

_____

Day 147

What part of your wedding vows mean the most to you?

Husband's answer:

_____
_____
_____
_____
_____
_____
_____
_____
_____
_____

Wife's answer:

_____
_____
_____
_____
_____
_____
_____
_____
_____
_____

Day 148

In your extended family, which relative did you really like?
Why?

Husband's answer:

_____

_____

_____

_____

_____

_____

_____

_____

_____

Wife's answer:

_____

_____

_____

_____

_____

_____

_____

_____

_____

Day 149

Who is/was your favorite world leader and why?

Husband's answer:

_____
_____
_____
_____
_____
_____
_____
_____
_____
_____

Wife's answer:

_____
_____
_____
_____
_____
_____
_____
_____
_____
_____

Day 150

Have you ever been baptized? What are your beliefs about baptism?

Husband's answer:

_____
_____
_____
_____
_____
_____
_____
_____
_____
_____

Wife's answer:

_____
_____
_____
_____
_____
_____
_____
_____
_____
_____

Day 151

What attracted you to your mate?

Husband's answer:

_____
_____
_____
_____
_____
_____
_____
_____
_____
_____

Wife's answer:

_____
_____
_____
_____
_____
_____
_____
_____
_____
_____

Day 152

If you passed away, what are three things you'd want your spouse to know?

Husband's answer:

_____
_____
_____
_____
_____
_____
_____
_____
_____
_____

Wife's answer:

_____
_____
_____
_____
_____
_____
_____
_____
_____
_____

Day 153

What is your favorite game?

Husband's answer:

_____

_____

_____

_____

_____

_____

_____

_____

_____

_____

Wife's answer:

_____

_____

_____

_____

_____

_____

_____

_____

_____

_____

Day 154

What theme has God been impressing on you lately?

Husband's answer:

_____
_____
_____
_____
_____
_____
_____
_____
_____
_____

Wife's answer:

_____
_____
_____
_____
_____
_____
_____
_____
_____
_____

Day 155

If your spouse had a superpower, what would it be?

Husband's answer:

_____

_____

_____

_____

_____

_____

_____

_____

_____

_____

Wife's answer:

_____

_____

_____

_____

_____

_____

_____

_____

_____

_____

Day 156

What product brand do you like?

Husband's answer:

_____
_____
_____
_____
_____
_____
_____
_____
_____
_____

Wife's answer:

_____
_____
_____
_____
_____
_____
_____
_____
_____
_____

Day 157

What is your favorite holiday?

Husband's answer:

_____
_____
_____
_____
_____
_____
_____
_____
_____
_____

Wife's answer:

_____
_____
_____
_____
_____
_____
_____
_____
_____

Day 158

How do you act when you're anxious?

Husband's answer:

_____
_____
_____
_____
_____
_____
_____
_____
_____
_____

Wife's answer:

_____
_____
_____
_____
_____
_____
_____
_____
_____
_____

Day 159

What person, outside of family, has influenced you the most?

Husband's answer:

_____
_____
_____
_____
_____
_____
_____
_____
_____
_____

Wife's answer:

_____
_____
_____
_____
_____
_____
_____
_____
_____
_____

Day 160

What do you think would be a good spiritual growth plan
for us over the next year?

Husband's answer:

_____
_____
_____
_____
_____
_____
_____
_____
_____
_____

Wife's answer:

_____
_____
_____
_____
_____
_____
_____
_____
_____
_____

Day 161

When was the last time you were concerned about your spouse?

Husband's answer:

_____

_____

_____

_____

_____

_____

_____

_____

_____

_____

Wife's answer:

_____

_____

_____

_____

_____

_____

_____

_____

_____

_____

Day 162

What have you discovered in the last year?

Husband's answer:

_____
_____
_____
_____
_____
_____
_____
_____
_____
_____

Wife's answer:

_____
_____
_____
_____
_____
_____
_____
_____
_____
_____

Day 163

How did you become a Christian?

Husband's answer:

_____

_____

_____

_____

_____

_____

_____

_____

_____

_____

_____

Wife's answer:

_____

_____

_____

_____

_____

_____

_____

_____

_____

_____

_____

Day 164

If you had unlimited resources, what would you give your spouse?

Husband's answer:

_____
_____
_____
_____
_____
_____
_____
_____
_____
_____

Wife's answer:

_____
_____
_____
_____
_____
_____
_____
_____
_____
_____

Day 165

Do you have a hero? Who is it?

Husband's answer:

_____
_____
_____
_____
_____
_____
_____
_____
_____
_____

Wife's answer:

_____
_____
_____
_____
_____
_____
_____
_____
_____
_____

Day 166

What are your top two prayer requests?

Husband's answer:

_____
_____
_____
_____
_____
_____
_____
_____
_____

Wife's answer:

_____
_____
_____
_____
_____
_____
_____
_____
_____

Day 167

What mode of transportation do you least enjoy?

Husband's answer:

_____
_____
_____
_____
_____
_____
_____
_____
_____
_____

Wife's answer:

_____
_____
_____
_____
_____
_____
_____
_____
_____
_____

Day 168

What was one of our best dates?

Husband's answer:

_____
_____
_____
_____
_____
_____
_____
_____
_____
_____

Wife's answer:

_____
_____
_____
_____
_____
_____
_____
_____
_____
_____

Day 169

What bothered you in the past month?

Husband's answer:

_____
_____
_____
_____
_____
_____
_____
_____
_____
_____

Wife's answer:

_____
_____
_____
_____
_____
_____
_____
_____
_____
_____

Day 170

What was the best year of our marriage and why?

Husband's answer:

_____
_____
_____
_____
_____
_____
_____
_____
_____
_____

Wife's answer:

_____
_____
_____
_____
_____
_____
_____
_____
_____
_____

Day 171

What is one of the proudest moments of your childhood or youth?

Husband's answer:

_____
_____
_____
_____
_____
_____
_____
_____
_____

Wife's answer:

_____
_____
_____
_____
_____
_____
_____
_____
_____

Day 172

How do you define love?

Husband's answer:

_____
_____
_____
_____
_____
_____
_____
_____
_____
_____
_____

Wife's answer:

_____
_____
_____
_____
_____
_____
_____
_____
_____
_____
_____

Day 173

When in your life did you persevere the most?

Husband's answer:

_____
_____
_____
_____
_____
_____
_____
_____
_____
_____

Wife's answer:

_____
_____
_____
_____
_____
_____
_____
_____
_____
_____

Day 174

What is one thing we can do to serve others outside our marriage?

Husband's answer:

_____
_____
_____
_____
_____
_____
_____
_____
_____
_____

Wife's answer:

_____
_____
_____
_____
_____
_____
_____
_____
_____
_____

Day 175

Were you nervous on your wedding day? When?

Husband's answer:

_____

_____

_____

_____

_____

_____

_____

_____

_____

_____

Wife's answer:

_____

_____

_____

_____

_____

_____

_____

_____

_____

_____

Day 176

What is your favorite hymn?

Husband's answer:

_____
_____
_____
_____
_____
_____
_____
_____
_____
_____

Wife's answer:

_____
_____
_____
_____
_____
_____
_____
_____
_____
_____

Day 177

What is your favorite memory from your wedding day?

Husband's answer:

_____
_____
_____
_____
_____
_____
_____
_____
_____
_____

Wife's answer:

_____
_____
_____
_____
_____
_____
_____
_____
_____
_____

Day 178

Have you ever been lost? When?

Husband's answer:

_____
_____
_____
_____
_____
_____
_____
_____
_____
_____

Wife's answer:

_____
_____
_____
_____
_____
_____
_____
_____
_____
_____

Day 179

What are your top priorities as a wife or husband?

Husband's answer:

_____
_____
_____
_____
_____
_____
_____
_____
_____
_____

Wife's answer:

_____
_____
_____
_____
_____
_____
_____
_____
_____
_____

Day 180

What is something you do differently from most people?

Husband's answer:

_____
_____
_____
_____
_____
_____
_____
_____
_____
_____

Wife's answer:

_____
_____
_____
_____
_____
_____
_____
_____
_____
_____

Day 181

How have you felt romanced by your spouse?

Husband's answer:

_____

_____

_____

_____

_____

_____

_____

_____

_____

_____

Wife's answer:

_____

_____

_____

_____

_____

_____

_____

_____

_____

_____

Day 182

What was your relationship(s) like with your siblings as you were growing up?

Husband's answer:

_____

_____

_____

_____

_____

_____

_____

_____

_____

_____

Wife's answer:

_____

_____

_____

_____

_____

_____

_____

_____

_____

_____

Day 183

What has surprised you positively in marriage?

Husband's answer:

_____
_____
_____
_____
_____
_____
_____
_____
_____
_____

Wife's answer:

_____
_____
_____
_____
_____
_____
_____
_____
_____
_____

Day 184

What is something you're looking forward to (excited about)?

Husband's answer:

_____
_____
_____
_____
_____
_____
_____
_____
_____
_____

Wife's answer:

_____
_____
_____
_____
_____
_____
_____
_____
_____
_____

Day 185

When was the last time someone disappointed you?

Husband's answer:

_____

_____

_____

_____

_____

_____

_____

_____

_____

_____

Wife's answer:

_____

_____

_____

_____

_____

_____

_____

_____

_____

_____

Day 186

When did you feel successful or accomplished?

Husband's answer:

_____
_____
_____
_____
_____
_____
_____
_____
_____
_____

Wife's answer:

_____
_____
_____
_____
_____
_____
_____
_____
_____
_____

Day 187

What is your favorite Bible verse?

Husband's answer:

_____
_____
_____
_____
_____
_____
_____
_____
_____
_____

Wife's answer:

_____
_____
_____
_____
_____
_____
_____
_____
_____
_____

Day 188

What topic do you wish our pastor would do a sermon series on?

Husband's answer:

_____
_____
_____
_____
_____
_____
_____
_____
_____
_____

Wife's answer:

_____
_____
_____
_____
_____
_____
_____
_____
_____
_____

Day 189

Did you ever go to camp growing up? If so, what was your experience like?

Husband's answer:

_____

_____

_____

_____

_____

_____

_____

_____

_____

Wife's answer:

_____

_____

_____

_____

_____

_____

_____

_____

_____

Day 190

What historical place would you like to visit?

Husband's answer:

_____

_____

_____

_____

_____

_____

_____

_____

_____

_____

Wife's answer:

_____

_____

_____

_____

_____

_____

_____

_____

_____

_____

Day 191

What has pleased you most in marriage?

Husband's answer:

_____
_____
_____
_____
_____
_____
_____
_____
_____
_____

Wife's answer:

_____
_____
_____
_____
_____
_____
_____
_____
_____
_____

Day 192

What do you want your legacy as a couple to be?

Husband's answer:

_____

_____

_____

_____

_____

_____

_____

_____

_____

_____

Wife's answer:

_____

_____

_____

_____

_____

_____

_____

_____

_____

_____

Day 193

What kind of church service connects best with you and why?

Husband's answer:

_____

_____

_____

_____

_____

_____

_____

_____

_____

Wife's answer:

_____

_____

_____

_____

_____

_____

_____

_____

_____

Day 194

Which of your mutual friends do you most trust to give your kids advice? Why?

Husband's answer:

_____
_____
_____
_____
_____
_____
_____
_____
_____
_____

Wife's answer:

_____
_____
_____
_____
_____
_____
_____
_____
_____
_____

Day 195

After high school, how did you decide on your college or vocational path?

Husband's answer:

_____
_____
_____
_____
_____
_____
_____
_____
_____

Wife's answer:

_____
_____
_____
_____
_____
_____
_____
_____
_____

Day 196

How can you be a better friend to your spouse?

Husband's answer:

_____
_____
_____
_____
_____
_____
_____
_____
_____
_____

Wife's answer:

_____
_____
_____
_____
_____
_____
_____
_____
_____
_____

Day 197

What is your favorite room in your home? Why?

Husband's answer:

_____
_____
_____
_____
_____
_____
_____
_____
_____
_____

Wife's answer:

_____
_____
_____
_____
_____
_____
_____
_____
_____
_____

Day 198

What kind of animal do you like to observe?

Husband's answer:

_____
_____
_____
_____
_____
_____
_____
_____
_____
_____

Wife's answer:

_____
_____
_____
_____
_____
_____
_____
_____
_____
_____

Day 199

What is the best advice you've ever received?

Husband's answer:

_____
_____
_____
_____
_____
_____
_____
_____
_____
_____

Wife's answer:

_____
_____
_____
_____
_____
_____
_____
_____
_____
_____

Day 200

What do you do when you are angry?

Husband's answer:

_____
_____
_____
_____
_____
_____
_____
_____
_____
_____

Wife's answer:

_____
_____
_____
_____
_____
_____
_____
_____
_____
_____

Day 201

What is something for which you'd be willing to splurge
and spend $1,000?

Husband's answer:

_____

_____

_____

_____

_____

_____

_____

_____

_____

Wife's answer:

_____

_____

_____

_____

_____

_____

_____

_____

_____

Day 202

How have you been hurt?

Husband's answer:

_____

_____

_____

_____

_____

_____

_____

_____

_____

_____

Wife's answer:

_____

_____

_____

_____

_____

_____

_____

_____

_____

_____

Day 203

What brings you peace?

Husband's answer:

_____
_____
_____
_____
_____
_____
_____
_____
_____
_____

Wife's answer:

_____
_____
_____
_____
_____
_____
_____
_____
_____
_____

Day 204

What is your favorite season and why?

Husband's answer:

_____
_____
_____
_____
_____
_____
_____
_____
_____
_____

Wife's answer:

_____
_____
_____
_____
_____
_____
_____
_____
_____
_____

Day 205

How often do you read the Bible?

Husband's answer:

_____

_____

_____

_____

_____

_____

_____

_____

_____

_____

Wife's answer:

_____

_____

_____

_____

_____

_____

_____

_____

_____

_____

Day 206

When we were dating, what date stands out as the most enjoyable one?

Husband's answer:

_____

_____

_____

_____

_____

_____

_____

_____

_____

_____

Wife's answer:

_____

_____

_____

_____

_____

_____

_____

_____

_____

_____

Day 207

What is something your spouse could teach you that would benefit your marriage?

Husband's answer:

_____
_____
_____
_____
_____
_____
_____
_____
_____

Wife's answer:

_____
_____
_____
_____
_____
_____
_____
_____
_____

Day 208

Who do you admire and why?

Husband's answer:

_____
_____
_____
_____
_____
_____
_____
_____
_____
_____

Wife's answer:

_____
_____
_____
_____
_____
_____
_____
_____
_____
_____

Day 209

Who would you call first in a crisis?

Husband's answer:

_____
_____
_____
_____
_____
_____
_____
_____
_____
_____

Wife's answer:

_____
_____
_____
_____
_____
_____
_____
_____
_____
_____

Day 210

Is there anyone at your job that you don't like to be around? Why?

Husband's answer:

_____
_____
_____
_____
_____
_____
_____
_____
_____
_____

Wife's answer:

_____
_____
_____
_____
_____
_____
_____
_____
_____
_____

Day 211

What is one hobby you'd like to try?

Husband's answer:

_____
_____
_____
_____
_____
_____
_____
_____
_____
_____

Wife's answer:

_____
_____
_____
_____
_____
_____
_____
_____
_____
_____

Day 212

Which appliance in our kitchen would it be the most difficult for you to live without?

Husband's answer:

_____
_____
_____
_____
_____
_____
_____
_____
_____
_____

Wife's answer:

_____
_____
_____
_____
_____
_____
_____
_____
_____
_____

Day 213

How are you motivated?

Husband's answer:

_____
_____
_____
_____
_____
_____
_____
_____
_____
_____
_____

Wife's answer:

_____
_____
_____
_____
_____
_____
_____
_____
_____
_____
_____

Day 214

What makes you afraid?

Husband's answer:

_____
_____
_____
_____
_____
_____
_____
_____
_____
_____

Wife's answer:

_____
_____
_____
_____
_____
_____
_____
_____
_____
_____

Day 215

What nationalities were your ancestors? Do you know?

Husband's answer:

_____
_____
_____
_____
_____
_____
_____
_____
_____
_____

Wife's answer:

_____
_____
_____
_____
_____
_____
_____
_____
_____
_____

Day 216

What are some of your favorite memories from growing up?

Husband's answer:

_____
_____
_____
_____
_____
_____
_____
_____
_____
_____

Wife's answer:

_____
_____
_____
_____
_____
_____
_____
_____
_____
_____

Day 217

How have you seen God answer prayer in your life?

Husband's answer:

_____
_____
_____
_____
_____
_____
_____
_____
_____
_____

Wife's answer:

_____
_____
_____
_____
_____
_____
_____
_____
_____
_____

Day 218

If money wasn't a factor, where would we go on vacation?

Husband's answer:

_____
_____
_____
_____
_____
_____
_____
_____
_____
_____

Wife's answer:

_____
_____
_____
_____
_____
_____
_____
_____
_____
_____

Day 219

When do you feel most loved by your spouse?

Husband's answer:

_____
_____
_____
_____
_____
_____
_____
_____
_____
_____

Wife's answer:

_____
_____
_____
_____
_____
_____
_____
_____
_____
_____

Day 220

What do you appreciate about your church?

Husband's answer:

_____
_____
_____
_____
_____
_____
_____
_____
_____
_____

Wife's answer:

_____
_____
_____
_____
_____
_____
_____
_____
_____
_____

Day 221

What skill set do you believe you need to acquire to advance your career?

Husband's answer:

_____
_____
_____
_____
_____
_____
_____
_____
_____

Wife's answer:

_____
_____
_____
_____
_____
_____
_____
_____
_____

Day 222

Were you ever bullied as a child or an adult?

Husband's answer:

_____

_____

_____

_____

_____

_____

_____

_____

_____

_____

Wife's answer:

_____

_____

_____

_____

_____

_____

_____

_____

_____

_____

Day 223

What is one of your favorite decorations in your home?

Husband's answer:

_____
_____
_____
_____
_____
_____
_____
_____
_____
_____

Wife's answer:

_____
_____
_____
_____
_____
_____
_____
_____
_____
_____

Day 224

Do you believe your budget is working well?
(If you don't have a budget, ask each other, "Do you
think we should have a budget?")

Husband's answer:

_____
_____
_____
_____
_____
_____
_____
_____
_____
_____

Wife's answer:

_____
_____
_____
_____
_____
_____
_____
_____
_____
_____

Day 225

What was difficult about your childhood?

Husband's answer:

_____
_____
_____
_____
_____
_____
_____
_____
_____
_____

Wife's answer:

_____
_____
_____
_____
_____
_____
_____
_____
_____
_____

Day 226

When was the last time you laughed really hard?

Husband's answer:

_____
_____
_____
_____
_____
_____
_____
_____
_____
_____

Wife's answer:

_____
_____
_____
_____
_____
_____
_____
_____
_____
_____

Day 227

What is your favorite book?

Husband's answer:

_____
_____
_____
_____
_____
_____
_____
_____
_____
_____

Wife's answer:

_____
_____
_____
_____
_____
_____
_____
_____
_____
_____

Day 228

What two people would you like to see reached for Christ?

Husband's answer:

_____
_____
_____
_____
_____
_____
_____
_____
_____
_____

Wife's answer:

_____
_____
_____
_____
_____
_____
_____
_____
_____
_____

Day 229

What is the biggest burden you are carrying right now?
How can your spouse support you?

Husband's answer:

_____

_____

_____

_____

_____

_____

_____

_____

_____

_____

Wife's answer:

_____

_____

_____

_____

_____

_____

_____

_____

_____

_____

Day 230

Do you ever feel under-appreciated at your job? Why?

Husband's answer:

_____
_____
_____
_____
_____
_____
_____
_____
_____
_____

Wife's answer:

_____
_____
_____
_____
_____
_____
_____
_____
_____
_____

Day 231

What's the funniest joke you can think of?

Husband's answer:

_____

_____

_____

_____

_____

_____

_____

_____

_____

_____

Wife's answer:

_____

_____

_____

_____

_____

_____

_____

_____

_____

_____

Day 232

What bad habit would you like to break?

Husband's answer:

_____
_____
_____
_____
_____
_____
_____
_____
_____
_____

Wife's answer:

_____
_____
_____
_____
_____
_____
_____
_____
_____
_____

Day 233

How has God blessed you recently?

Husband's answer:

_____
_____
_____
_____
_____
_____
_____
_____
_____
_____

Wife's answer:

_____
_____
_____
_____
_____
_____
_____
_____
_____
_____

Day 234

Have you ever witnessed something you can't explain?

Husband's answer:

_____

_____

_____

_____

_____

_____

_____

_____

_____

_____

Wife's answer:

_____

_____

_____

_____

_____

_____

_____

_____

_____

_____

Day 235

Where would you like to retire?

Husband's answer:

_____
_____
_____
_____
_____
_____
_____
_____
_____
_____

Wife's answer:

_____
_____
_____
_____
_____
_____
_____
_____
_____
_____

Day 236

Is there anyone at your job you admire? Why?

Husband's answer:

_____
_____
_____
_____
_____
_____
_____
_____
_____
_____

Wife's answer:

_____
_____
_____
_____
_____
_____
_____
_____
_____
_____

Day 237

What would you like to experience that you haven't?

Husband's answer:

_____
_____
_____
_____
_____
_____
_____
_____
_____
_____
_____

Wife's answer:

_____
_____
_____
_____
_____
_____
_____
_____
_____
_____
_____

Day 238

Who is your best same-gender friend and why?

Husband's answer:

_____
_____
_____
_____
_____
_____
_____
_____
_____
_____

Wife's answer:

_____
_____
_____
_____
_____
_____
_____
_____
_____
_____

Day 239

Where do we need to trust God more in our marriage?

Husband's answer:

_____
_____
_____
_____
_____
_____
_____
_____
_____
_____

Wife's answer:

_____
_____
_____
_____
_____
_____
_____
_____
_____
_____

Day 240

What can you do to better express appreciation to your spouse?

Husband's answer:

_____
_____
_____
_____
_____
_____
_____
_____
_____
_____

Wife's answer:

_____
_____
_____
_____
_____
_____
_____
_____
_____
_____

Day 241

What is your best memory from grade school?

Husband's answer:

_____
_____
_____
_____
_____
_____
_____
_____
_____
_____

Wife's answer:

_____
_____
_____
_____
_____
_____
_____
_____
_____
_____

Day 242

What is your favorite holiday tradition?

Husband's answer:

_____
_____
_____
_____
_____
_____
_____
_____
_____
_____

Wife's answer:

_____
_____
_____
_____
_____
_____
_____
_____
_____
_____

Day 243

What would you like to do to improve your relationship with God?

Husband's answer:

_____
_____
_____
_____
_____
_____
_____
_____
_____
_____
_____

Wife's answer:

_____
_____
_____
_____
_____
_____
_____
_____
_____
_____
_____

Day 244

As we age, what concerns do you have?

Husband's answer:

_____
_____
_____
_____
_____
_____
_____
_____
_____
_____

Wife's answer:

_____
_____
_____
_____
_____
_____
_____
_____
_____
_____

Day 245

What overwhelms you right now?

Husband's answer:

_____
_____
_____
_____
_____
_____
_____
_____
_____
_____

Wife's answer:

_____
_____
_____
_____
_____
_____
_____
_____
_____
_____

Day 246

What is your favorite color of clothing to wear?

Husband's answer:

_____
_____
_____
_____
_____
_____
_____
_____
_____
_____

Wife's answer:

_____
_____
_____
_____
_____
_____
_____
_____
_____
_____

Day 247

How would you describe what heaven is like?
What do you look forward to there?

Husband's answer:

_____

_____

_____

_____

_____

_____

_____

_____

_____

Wife's answer:

_____

_____

_____

_____

_____

_____

_____

_____

_____

Day 248

From start to finish, what would be a great romantic date?

Husband's answer:

_____
_____
_____
_____
_____
_____
_____
_____
_____
_____
_____

Wife's answer:

_____
_____
_____
_____
_____
_____
_____
_____
_____
_____
_____

Day 249

What is something you're particular about?

Husband's answer:

_____
_____
_____
_____
_____
_____
_____
_____
_____
_____

Wife's answer:

_____
_____
_____
_____
_____
_____
_____
_____
_____
_____

Day 250

What is your favorite dessert?

Husband's answer:

_____
_____
_____
_____
_____
_____
_____
_____
_____
_____

Wife's answer:

_____
_____
_____
_____
_____
_____
_____
_____
_____
_____

Day 251

How can you help alleviate worry in your spouse's life?

Husband's answer:

_____
_____
_____
_____
_____
_____
_____
_____
_____
_____

Wife's answer:

_____
_____
_____
_____
_____
_____
_____
_____
_____
_____

Day 252

What is the most interesting thing you learned in the past week?

Husband's answer:

_____

_____

_____

_____

_____

_____

_____

_____

_____

_____

Wife's answer:

_____

_____

_____

_____

_____

_____

_____

_____

_____

_____

Day 253

What next steps can we take to grow together spiritually?

Husband's answer:

_____
_____
_____
_____
_____
_____
_____
_____
_____
_____

Wife's answer:

_____
_____
_____
_____
_____
_____
_____
_____
_____
_____

Day 254

When did you feel totally awkward and out of place?

Husband's answer:

_____
_____
_____
_____
_____
_____
_____
_____
_____
_____

Wife's answer:

_____
_____
_____
_____
_____
_____
_____
_____
_____
_____

Day 255

Are you more like your mom or dad? Why?

Husband's answer:

_____

_____

_____

_____

_____

_____

_____

_____

_____

_____

Wife's answer:

_____

_____

_____

_____

_____

_____

_____

_____

_____

_____

Day 256

Who has influenced you the most spiritually and how?

Husband's answer:

_____
_____
_____
_____
_____
_____
_____
_____
_____
_____

Wife's answer:

_____
_____
_____
_____
_____
_____
_____
_____
_____
_____

Day 257

How can you improve your conflict resolution with your spouse?

Husband's answer:

_____
_____
_____
_____
_____
_____
_____
_____
_____
_____

Wife's answer:

_____
_____
_____
_____
_____
_____
_____
_____
_____
_____

Day 258

What do you take for granted?

Husband's answer:

_____
_____
_____
_____
_____
_____
_____
_____
_____
_____

Wife's answer:

_____
_____
_____
_____
_____
_____
_____
_____
_____
_____

Day 259

What do you do that you'd like your spouse to watch or join you in?

Husband's answer:

_____
_____
_____
_____
_____
_____
_____
_____
_____
_____
_____

Wife's answer:

_____
_____
_____
_____
_____
_____
_____
_____
_____
_____
_____

Day 260

What is something about yourself you'd like to change?

Husband's answer:

_____
_____
_____
_____
_____
_____
_____
_____
_____
_____

Wife's answer:

_____
_____
_____
_____
_____
_____
_____
_____
_____
_____

Day 261

How are our differences a strength in our marriage?

Husband's answer:

_____
_____
_____
_____
_____
_____
_____
_____
_____
_____
_____

Wife's answer:

_____
_____
_____
_____
_____
_____
_____
_____
_____
_____
_____

Day 262

What is a dream you have for you and your spouse?

Husband's answer:

_____
_____
_____
_____
_____
_____
_____
_____
_____
_____

Wife's answer:

_____
_____
_____
_____
_____
_____
_____
_____
_____
_____

Day 263

What is one of your biggest pet peeves?

Husband's answer:

_____
_____
_____
_____
_____
_____
_____
_____
_____
_____

Wife's answer:

_____
_____
_____
_____
_____
_____
_____
_____
_____
_____

Day 264

What qualities make a great wife?

Husband's answer:

_____

_____

_____

_____

_____

_____

_____

_____

_____

_____

Wife's answer:

_____

_____

_____

_____

_____

_____

_____

_____

_____

_____

Day 265

What good habits do you practice?

Husband's answer:

_____

_____

_____

_____

_____

_____

_____

_____

_____

_____

Wife's answer:

_____

_____

_____

_____

_____

_____

_____

_____

_____

_____

Day 266

What is the craziest thing we've ever done?

Husband's answer:

_____

_____

_____

_____

_____

_____

_____

_____

_____

_____

Wife's answer:

_____

_____

_____

_____

_____

_____

_____

_____

_____

_____

Day 267

Are we too busy, not busy enough, or just right?

Husband's answer:

_____
_____
_____
_____
_____
_____
_____
_____
_____
_____

Wife's answer:

_____
_____
_____
_____
_____
_____
_____
_____
_____
_____

Day 268

What is hard for you?

Husband's answer:

_____
_____
_____
_____
_____
_____
_____
_____
_____
_____

Wife's answer:

_____
_____
_____
_____
_____
_____
_____
_____
_____
_____

Day 269

How has your spouse made you a better person?

Husband's answer:

_____
_____
_____
_____
_____
_____
_____
_____
_____
_____

Wife's answer:

_____
_____
_____
_____
_____
_____
_____
_____
_____
_____

Day 270

What is the longest time period that you've gone without sleep?

Husband's answer:

_____
_____
_____
_____
_____
_____
_____
_____
_____
_____
_____

Wife's answer:

_____
_____
_____
_____
_____
_____
_____
_____
_____
_____
_____

Day 271

How could you serve your spouse?

Husband's answer:

_____
_____
_____
_____
_____
_____
_____
_____
_____
_____

Wife's answer:

_____
_____
_____
_____
_____
_____
_____
_____
_____
_____

Day 272

What is one of the best surprises you've ever had?

Husband's answer:

_____
_____
_____
_____
_____
_____
_____
_____
_____
_____

Wife's answer:

_____
_____
_____
_____
_____
_____
_____
_____
_____
_____

Day 273

What can you do to make your spouse feel more loved?

Husband's answer:

_____
_____
_____
_____
_____
_____
_____
_____
_____
_____

Wife's answer:

_____
_____
_____
_____
_____
_____
_____
_____
_____
_____

Day 274

What has been difficult for you in your marriage?

Husband's answer:

_____
_____
_____
_____
_____
_____
_____
_____
_____
_____

Wife's answer:

_____
_____
_____
_____
_____
_____
_____
_____
_____
_____

Day 275

When was the last time you disappointed someone?

Husband's answer:

_____
_____
_____
_____
_____
_____
_____
_____
_____

Wife's answer:

_____
_____
_____
_____
_____
_____
_____
_____
_____

Day 276

How can we create more joy in our marriage?

Husband's answer:

_____
_____
_____
_____
_____
_____
_____
_____
_____
_____

Wife's answer:

_____
_____
_____
_____
_____
_____
_____
_____
_____
_____

Day 277

What is your favorite meal?

Husband's answer:

_____
_____
_____
_____
_____
_____
_____
_____
_____
_____

Wife's answer:

_____
_____
_____
_____
_____
_____
_____
_____
_____
_____

Day 278

Do you believe in miracles today? Why or why not?

Husband's answer:

_____
_____
_____
_____
_____
_____
_____
_____
_____
_____

Wife's answer:

_____
_____
_____
_____
_____
_____
_____
_____
_____
_____

Day 279

What project can we do together?

Husband's answer:

_____
_____
_____
_____
_____
_____
_____
_____
_____
_____

Wife's answer:

_____
_____
_____
_____
_____
_____
_____
_____
_____
_____

Day 280

What is your favorite memory from our honeymoon?

Husband's answer:

_____
_____
_____
_____
_____
_____
_____
_____
_____
_____

Wife's answer:

_____
_____
_____
_____
_____
_____
_____
_____
_____

Day 281

When is your favorite time of day to make love?

Husband's answer:

_____
_____
_____
_____
_____
_____
_____
_____
_____
_____

Wife's answer:

_____
_____
_____
_____
_____
_____
_____
_____
_____
_____

Day 282

Who did you look up to or admire when you were growing up?

Husband's answer:

_____

_____

_____

_____

_____

_____

_____

_____

_____

_____

Wife's answer:

_____

_____

_____

_____

_____

_____

_____

_____

_____

_____

Day 283

If you needed to hear a convicting sermon, what would the topic be?

Husband's answer:

_____
_____
_____
_____
_____
_____
_____
_____
_____
_____

Wife's answer:

_____
_____
_____
_____
_____
_____
_____
_____
_____
_____

Day 284

Do any of your mutual friends make you uncomfortable? How?

Husband's answer:

_____
_____
_____
_____
_____
_____
_____
_____
_____
_____

Wife's answer:

_____
_____
_____
_____
_____
_____
_____
_____
_____
_____

Day 285

What qualities make a good boss?

Husband's answer:

_____
_____
_____
_____
_____
_____
_____
_____
_____
_____
_____

Wife's answer:

_____
_____
_____
_____
_____
_____
_____
_____
_____
_____
_____

Day 286

When was the last time you did something you didn't want to do?

Husband's answer:

_____
_____
_____
_____
_____
_____
_____
_____
_____
_____

Wife's answer:

_____
_____
_____
_____
_____
_____
_____
_____
_____
_____

Day 287

What household chore do you enjoy doing?

Husband's answer:

_____
_____
_____
_____
_____
_____
_____
_____
_____
_____

Wife's answer:

_____
_____
_____
_____
_____
_____
_____
_____
_____
_____

Day 288

What is your favorite time of the day?

Husband's answer:

_____
_____
_____
_____
_____
_____
_____
_____
_____
_____

Wife's answer:

_____
_____
_____
_____
_____
_____
_____
_____
_____
_____

Day 289

What would you like to do with your grandchildren?

Husband's answer:

_____
_____
_____
_____
_____
_____
_____
_____
_____
_____

Wife's answer:

_____
_____
_____
_____
_____
_____
_____
_____
_____
_____

Day 290

How do you know when your spouse is angry?

Husband's answer:

_____
_____
_____
_____
_____
_____
_____
_____
_____
_____

Wife's answer:

_____
_____
_____
_____
_____
_____
_____
_____
_____
_____

Day 291

How could we manage money better?

Husband's answer:

_____

_____

_____

_____

_____

_____

_____

_____

_____

_____

Wife's answer:

_____

_____

_____

_____

_____

_____

_____

_____

_____

_____

_____

Day 292

When were you most recently afraid?

Husband's answer:

_____

_____

_____

_____

_____

_____

_____

_____

_____

_____

Wife's answer:

_____

_____

_____

_____

_____

_____

_____

_____

_____

_____

Day 293

When were you unexpectedly blessed?

Husband's answer:

_____
_____
_____
_____
_____
_____
_____
_____
_____
_____

Wife's answer:

_____
_____
_____
_____
_____
_____
_____
_____
_____
_____

Day 294

What is your least favorite household chore?

Husband's answer:

_____
_____
_____
_____
_____
_____
_____
_____
_____
_____

Wife's answer:

_____
_____
_____
_____
_____
_____
_____
_____
_____
_____

Day 295

If you could sit down with Jesus today, what would you like to ask him?

Husband's answer:

_____
_____
_____
_____
_____
_____
_____
_____
_____
_____

Wife's answer:

_____
_____
_____
_____
_____
_____
_____
_____
_____
_____

Day 296

If you had an hour to waste today, what would you do?

Husband's answer:

_____
_____
_____
_____
_____
_____
_____
_____
_____
_____

Wife's answer:

_____
_____
_____
_____
_____
_____
_____
_____
_____
_____

Day 297

How do you sacrifice for your spouse?

Husband's answer:

_____
_____
_____
_____
_____
_____
_____
_____
_____
_____

Wife's answer:

_____
_____
_____
_____
_____
_____
_____
_____
_____
_____

Day 298

Who is someone you admire who treats his/her spouse well?

Husband's answer:

_____
_____
_____
_____
_____
_____
_____
_____
_____
_____

Wife's answer:

_____
_____
_____
_____
_____
_____
_____
_____
_____
_____

Day 299

When was the last time you were mad at a friend? Why?

Husband's answer:

_____
_____
_____
_____
_____
_____
_____
_____
_____
_____

Wife's answer:

_____
_____
_____
_____
_____
_____
_____
_____
_____
_____

Day 300

What is your least favorite aspect of your job?

Husband's answer:

_____

_____

_____

_____

_____

_____

_____

_____

_____

_____

Wife's answer:

_____

_____

_____

_____

_____

_____

_____

_____

_____

_____

Day 301

What skill do you wish you had?

Husband's answer:

_____

_____

_____

_____

_____

_____

_____

_____

_____

Wife's answer:

_____

_____

_____

_____

_____

_____

_____

_____

_____

Day 302

How could we be better neighbors?

Husband's answer:

_____
_____
_____
_____
_____
_____
_____
_____
_____
_____

Wife's answer:

_____
_____
_____
_____
_____
_____
_____
_____
_____
_____

Day 303

What should be our financial priorities?

Husband's answer:

_____
_____
_____
_____
_____
_____
_____
_____
_____
_____

Wife's answer:

_____
_____
_____
_____
_____
_____
_____
_____
_____
_____

Day 304

When were you recently discouraged?

Husband's answer:

_____

_____

_____

_____

_____

_____

_____

_____

_____

_____

Wife's answer:

_____

_____

_____

_____

_____

_____

_____

_____

_____

_____

Day 305

How would you like to influence your children?

Husband's answer:

_____

_____

_____

_____

_____

_____

_____

_____

_____

_____

Wife's answer:

_____

_____

_____

_____

_____

_____

_____

_____

_____

_____

Day 306

Where is your favorite spot to sit in our home?

Husband's answer:

_____
_____
_____
_____
_____
_____
_____
_____
_____
_____

Wife's answer:

_____
_____
_____
_____
_____
_____
_____
_____
_____
_____

Day 307

What is your opinion of the spiritual discipline of fasting?

Husband's answer:

_____
_____
_____
_____
_____
_____
_____
_____
_____

Wife's answer:

_____
_____
_____
_____
_____
_____
_____
_____
_____

Day 308

What place(s) are on your travel bucket list?

Husband's answer:

_____
_____
_____
_____
_____
_____
_____
_____
_____
_____

Wife's answer:

_____
_____
_____
_____
_____
_____
_____
_____
_____
_____

Day 309

What would please you sexually?

Husband's answer:

_____
_____
_____
_____
_____
_____
_____
_____
_____
_____

Wife's answer:

_____
_____
_____
_____
_____
_____
_____
_____
_____
_____

Day 310

With which two couples would you like to become better friends?

Husband's answer:

_____
_____
_____
_____
_____
_____
_____
_____
_____
_____

Wife's answer:

_____
_____
_____
_____
_____
_____
_____
_____
_____
_____

Day 311

What is your dream environment in which to work?

Husband's answer:

_____
_____
_____
_____
_____
_____
_____
_____
_____
_____

Wife's answer:

_____
_____
_____
_____
_____
_____
_____
_____
_____
_____

Day 312

What is your favorite article of clothing? Why?

Husband's answer:

_____
_____
_____
_____
_____
_____
_____
_____
_____
_____

Wife's answer:

_____
_____
_____
_____
_____
_____
_____
_____
_____
_____

Day 313

If a disaster struck your home, what three items would you grab?

Husband's answer:

_____
_____
_____
_____
_____
_____
_____
_____
_____
_____

Wife's answer:

_____
_____
_____
_____
_____
_____
_____
_____
_____
_____

Day 314

What home improvement project do we need to save for and complete?

Husband's answer:

_____
_____
_____
_____
_____
_____
_____
_____
_____
_____

Wife's answer:

_____
_____
_____
_____
_____
_____
_____
_____
_____
_____

Day 315

When were you embarrassed?

Husband's answer:

_____
_____
_____
_____
_____
_____
_____
_____
_____
_____

Wife's answer:

_____
_____
_____
_____
_____
_____
_____
_____
_____
_____

Day 316

When were you affirmed in life?

Husband's answer:

_____
_____
_____
_____
_____
_____
_____
_____
_____
_____

Wife's answer:

_____
_____
_____
_____
_____
_____
_____
_____
_____
_____

Day 317

What is your favorite restaurant?

Husband's answer:

_____

_____

_____

_____

_____

_____

_____

_____

_____

_____

Wife's answer:

_____

_____

_____

_____

_____

_____

_____

_____

_____

_____

Day 318

How can you help your spouse grow closer to the Lord?

Husband's answer:

_____
_____
_____
_____
_____
_____
_____
_____
_____
_____

Wife's answer:

_____
_____
_____
_____
_____
_____
_____
_____
_____
_____

Day 319

What do you desire for our marriage to become?

Husband's answer:

_____

_____

_____

_____

_____

_____

_____

_____

_____

_____

Wife's answer:

_____

_____

_____

_____

_____

_____

_____

_____

_____

_____

Day 320

What would you like to be doing in 10 years when you think of your career?

Husband's answer:

_____
_____
_____
_____
_____
_____
_____
_____
_____
_____

Wife's answer:

_____
_____
_____
_____
_____
_____
_____
_____
_____
_____

Day 321

What does your spouse do that annoys you?

Husband's answer:

_____

_____

_____

_____

_____

_____

_____

_____

_____

_____

Wife's answer:

_____

_____

_____

_____

_____

_____

_____

_____

_____

_____

Day 322

Who do you miss that has died?

Husband's answer:

_____
_____
_____
_____
_____
_____
_____
_____
_____
_____

Wife's answer:

_____
_____
_____
_____
_____
_____
_____
_____
_____
_____

Day 323

What is your favorite type of ethnic food?

Husband's answer:

_____

_____

_____

_____

_____

_____

_____

_____

_____

_____

Wife's answer:

_____

_____

_____

_____

_____

_____

_____

_____

_____

_____

Day 324

What temptation do you struggle with the most?

Husband's answer:

_____
_____
_____
_____
_____
_____
_____
_____
_____
_____

Wife's answer:

_____
_____
_____
_____
_____
_____
_____
_____
_____
_____

Day 325

When was one of the best seasons of our marriage?

Husband's answer:

_____
_____
_____
_____
_____
_____
_____
_____
_____
_____

Wife's answer:

_____
_____
_____
_____
_____
_____
_____
_____
_____
_____

Day 326

What is something you look forward to in your current job?

Husband's answer:

_____
_____
_____
_____
_____
_____
_____
_____
_____

Wife's answer:

_____
_____
_____
_____
_____
_____
_____
_____
_____

Day 327

What is something you're not very good at?

Husband's answer:

_____
_____
_____
_____
_____
_____
_____
_____
_____
_____

Wife's answer:

_____
_____
_____
_____
_____
_____
_____
_____
_____
_____

Day 328

If money wasn't a consideration, what vehicle would you drive?

Husband's answer:

_____
_____
_____
_____
_____
_____
_____
_____
_____
_____

Wife's answer:

_____
_____
_____
_____
_____
_____
_____
_____
_____
_____

Day 329

Are you satisfied with the amount of spiritual involvement
we have at our church? Why or why not?

Husband's answer:

_____
_____
_____
_____
_____
_____
_____
_____
_____
_____

Wife's answer:

_____
_____
_____
_____
_____
_____
_____
_____
_____
_____

Day 330

What adventure would you like to experience with your spouse?

Husband's answer:

_____
_____
_____
_____
_____
_____
_____
_____
_____
_____

Wife's answer:

_____
_____
_____
_____
_____
_____
_____
_____
_____
_____

Day 331

What is your worst memory from grade school?

Husband's answer:

_____

_____

_____

_____

_____

_____

_____

_____

_____

Wife's answer:

_____

_____

_____

_____

_____

_____

_____

_____

_____

Day 332

What Bible verse has impacted you and why?

Husband's answer:

_____
_____
_____
_____
_____
_____
_____
_____
_____
_____

Wife's answer:

_____
_____
_____
_____
_____
_____
_____
_____
_____
_____

Day 333

What spiritual goals do you have and how do you plan to accomplish them?

Husband's answer:

_____
_____
_____
_____
_____
_____
_____
_____
_____
_____

Wife's answer:

_____
_____
_____
_____
_____
_____
_____
_____
_____
_____

Day 334

Besides your spouse, what is one thing you will never get rid of?

Husband's answer:

_____
_____
_____
_____
_____
_____
_____
_____
_____
_____

Wife's answer:

_____
_____
_____
_____
_____
_____
_____
_____
_____
_____

Day 335

When did you quit something and later wished you hadn't?

Husband's answer:

_____
_____
_____
_____
_____
_____
_____
_____
_____
_____

Wife's answer:

_____
_____
_____
_____
_____
_____
_____
_____
_____
_____

Day 336

What is your favorite TV series?

Husband's answer:

_____
_____
_____
_____
_____
_____
_____
_____
_____
_____
_____

Wife's answer:

_____
_____
_____
_____
_____
_____
_____
_____
_____
_____
_____

Day 337

What are your thoughts on hell?

Husband's answer:

_____
_____
_____
_____
_____
_____
_____
_____
_____
_____

Wife's answer:

_____
_____
_____
_____
_____
_____
_____
_____
_____
_____

Day 338

What is a date you'd like to experience in the next 3 months? How can we make it happen?

Husband's answer:

_____
_____
_____
_____
_____
_____
_____
_____
_____
_____

Wife's answer:

_____
_____
_____
_____
_____
_____
_____
_____
_____
_____

Day 339

Do you think your parents were too lenient, too strict or just right? Why?

Husband's answer:

_____
_____
_____
_____
_____
_____
_____
_____
_____
_____

Wife's answer:

_____
_____
_____
_____
_____
_____
_____
_____
_____
_____

Day 340

What's something you'd like to change in your marriage?

Husband's answer:

_____
_____
_____
_____
_____
_____
_____
_____
_____
_____

Wife's answer:

_____
_____
_____
_____
_____
_____
_____
_____
_____
_____

Day 341

What prayer has the Lord answered for you recently?

Husband's answer:

_____
_____
_____
_____
_____
_____
_____
_____
_____
_____

Wife's answer:

_____
_____
_____
_____
_____
_____
_____
_____
_____
_____

Day 342

What are your dreams for your family?

Husband's answer:

_____
_____
_____
_____
_____
_____
_____
_____
_____
_____

Wife's answer:

_____
_____
_____
_____
_____
_____
_____
_____
_____
_____

Day 343

How are you selfish?

Husband's answer:

_____
_____
_____
_____
_____
_____
_____
_____
_____

Wife's answer:

_____
_____
_____
_____
_____
_____
_____
_____
_____

Day 344

Is there anything for which you need to ask your spouse's forgiveness?

Husband's answer:

_____
_____
_____
_____
_____
_____
_____
_____
_____
_____

Wife's answer:

_____
_____
_____
_____
_____
_____
_____
_____
_____
_____

Day 345

When were you proud of your spouse?

Husband's answer:

_____

_____

_____

_____

_____

_____

_____

_____

_____

Wife's answer:

_____

_____

_____

_____

_____

_____

_____

_____

_____

Day 346

What did you collect as a child?

Husband's answer:

_____
_____
_____
_____
_____
_____
_____
_____
_____
_____

Wife's answer:

_____
_____
_____
_____
_____
_____
_____
_____
_____
_____

Day 347

What's your favorite book of the Bible?

Husband's answer:

_____
_____
_____
_____
_____
_____
_____
_____
_____
_____

Wife's answer:

_____
_____
_____
_____
_____
_____
_____
_____
_____
_____

Day 348

When did you know you wanted to marry your spouse?

Husband's answer:

_____

_____

_____

_____

_____

_____

_____

_____

_____

_____

Wife's answer:

_____

_____

_____

_____

_____

_____

_____

_____

_____

_____

Day 349

What is something you do every day?

Husband's answer:

_____

_____

_____

_____

_____

_____

_____

_____

_____

Wife's answer:

_____

_____

_____

_____

_____

_____

_____

_____

_____

Day 350

Do we have any unresolved conflict?

Husband's answer:

_____
_____
_____
_____
_____
_____
_____
_____
_____
_____

Wife's answer:

_____
_____
_____
_____
_____
_____
_____
_____
_____
_____

Day 351

What is the most disgusting food you've ever eaten?

Husband's answer:

_____
_____
_____
_____
_____
_____
_____
_____
_____

Wife's answer:

_____
_____
_____
_____
_____
_____
_____
_____
_____

Day 352

What is your favorite part of your spouse's body?

Husband's answer:

_____
_____
_____
_____
_____
_____
_____
_____
_____
_____

Wife's answer:

_____
_____
_____
_____
_____
_____
_____
_____
_____
_____

Day 353

When did you most recently feel proud?

Husband's answer:

_____
_____
_____
_____
_____
_____
_____
_____
_____
_____

Wife's answer:

_____
_____
_____
_____
_____
_____
_____
_____
_____
_____

Day 354

When are we at our best maritally?

Husband's answer:

_____

_____

_____

_____

_____

_____

_____

_____

_____

_____

Wife's answer:

_____

_____

_____

_____

_____

_____

_____

_____

_____

_____

Day 355

Do you tend to look more at the past or the future?

Husband's answer:

_____
_____
_____
_____
_____
_____
_____
_____
_____
_____

Wife's answer:

_____
_____
_____
_____
_____
_____
_____
_____
_____
_____

Day 356

How can we build our marriage?

Husband's answer:

_____
_____
_____
_____
_____
_____
_____
_____
_____
_____

Wife's answer:

_____
_____
_____
_____
_____
_____
_____
_____
_____
_____

Day 357

What item on your "bucket list" might happen in the next one or two years?

Husband's answer:

_____
_____
_____
_____
_____
_____
_____
_____
_____
_____

Wife's answer:

_____
_____
_____
_____
_____
_____
_____
_____
_____
_____

Day 358

What is something your spouse can't live without?

Husband's answer:

_____

_____

_____

_____

_____

_____

_____

_____

_____

_____

Wife's answer:

_____

_____

_____

_____

_____

_____

_____

_____

_____

_____

Day 359

What surprised you the most on your wedding day?

Husband's answer:

_____

_____

_____

_____

_____

_____

_____

_____

_____

_____

Wife's answer:

_____

_____

_____

_____

_____

_____

_____

_____

_____

_____

Day 360

What do you miss from your childhood?

Husband's answer:

_____
_____
_____
_____
_____
_____
_____
_____
_____
_____
_____

Wife's answer:

_____
_____
_____
_____
_____
_____
_____
_____
_____
_____
_____

Day 361

What do you want your marriage to look like in 10 years?

Husband's answer:

_____
_____
_____
_____
_____
_____
_____
_____
_____
_____
_____

Wife's answer:

_____
_____
_____
_____
_____
_____
_____
_____
_____
_____
_____

Day 362

What makes you feel pampered?

Husband's answer:

_____
_____
_____
_____
_____
_____
_____
_____
_____
_____

Wife's answer:

_____
_____
_____
_____
_____
_____
_____
_____
_____
_____

Day 363

What is one word you would use to describe your spouse?
Explain.

Husband's answer:

_____
_____
_____
_____
_____
_____
_____
_____
_____
_____

Wife's answer:

_____
_____
_____
_____
_____
_____
_____
_____
_____
_____

Day 364

What would you like to accomplish in the next year?

Husband's answer:

_____
_____
_____
_____
_____
_____
_____
_____
_____
_____
_____

Wife's answer:

_____
_____
_____
_____
_____
_____
_____
_____
_____
_____
_____

Day 365

What is something your spouse needs from you in your marriage?

Husband's answer:

_____

_____

_____

_____

_____

_____

_____

_____

_____

_____

_____

Wife's answer:

_____

_____

_____

_____

_____

_____

_____

_____

_____

_____

_____

Day 366

Where do you think we've let our guard down when it comes to protecting our marriage?

Husband's answer:

_____
_____
_____
_____
_____
_____
_____
_____
_____
_____

Wife's answer:

_____
_____
_____
_____
_____
_____
_____
_____
_____
_____

Connect with us!

 BuildYourMarriage.org

 Facebook.com/BuildYourMarriage

 @BuildUrMarriage

 BuildYourMarriage

Also from Build Your Marriage:

Learn about couples of the Bible and the real-life issues they faced in this nine session small group study. Available for download or purchase wherever books are sold.

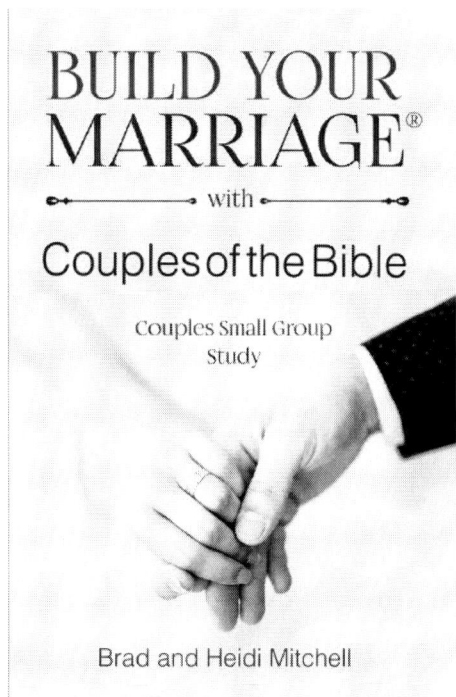